The Cook Book

Fiona Munro

Illustrated by Nick Sharratt

FAMILY LEARNING

Kitchen Rules

Before you start, roll up your sleeves and put on an apron. Then wash your hands.

Get out everything you will need for a recipe before you start cooking.

Clear up as you work. Wipe up any spills straight away.

When you have finished, remember to wash up.

Ask an adult to help when:

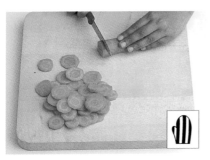

Cutting and slicing

Weighing and measuring

Using the oven

Look out for these symbols:

 Ask an adult to help.

 Turn on the oven, with help from an adult.

Giant Rolls

You will need:

fork

sharp knife

table knife

tablespoon

mixing bowls

chopping board

butter

different kinds of rolls

To make egg and salami rolls, you will need:

2 hard-boiled eggs

cress

1 tablespoon of mayonnaise

a pinch of salt

black pepper

salami

Try these fillings for the other rolls:

tomato

lettuce

cheese

ham

tuna

① Tap the eggs on the worktop, then peel off the cracked shells. Wash off any bits of shell left on the eggs.

② In a clean bowl, mash the eggs with a fork. Mix in the cress, mayonnaise, salt and black pepper.

③ On the chopping board, cut a roll in half with the sharp knife. Spread a little butter onto each half.

④ Spread a spoonful of the egg mixture evenly over the botton half of the roll.

⑤ Take three slices of salami. Fold each in half, then in half again. Put this on top of the egg mixture.

⑥ Cover with the top half of the roll.

Your giant rolls could look like these:

Tuna roll

Ham and cheese roll

Egg and salami roll

Mini Pizzas

You will need:

baking tray

chopping board

teaspoon

bread knife

 180°C, 350°F, Gas Mark 4

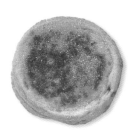

1 muffin for
each person

tomato
ketchup

mozzarella or
cheddar cheese

Choose from these toppings:

ham

mushrooms

olives

tuna

tomato

red pepper

pepperoni

① On the chopping board, cut the muffins in half with the bread knife.

② Spread a spoonful of tomato ketchup onto each half.

③ Lay the cheese on top. Cover with your choice of toppings.

④ Put the mini pizzas on the baking tray.

⑤ Cook the mini pizzas for 10 minutes. When the cheese is melted and bubbling, they are ready.

Your mini pizzas could look like these:

Tuna pizza

Cheese and
ham pizza

Pepperoni pizza

Fruit Fools

You will need:

whisk

fork

tablespoon

mixing bowls

serving dishes

200g (8oz) strawberries

or 2 small bananas

¼ litre (½ pint) double
cream **or** yoghurt

25g (1oz)
caster sugar

Decorate your fruit fools using:

chocolate chips

biscuits

seedless grapes

glacé cherries

kiwi fruit

strawberries

1 If you are using cream, whisk it until it is thick.

2 Use the fork to mash the strawberries or bananas until smooth. (If you use bananas, add a few drops of lemon juice to stop them going brown.)

3 Use the spoon to stir the cream or yoghurt into the fruit. Add the caster sugar.

4 Spoon the mixture into serving dishes. Decorate your fruit fools.

Your fruit fools could look like these:

Bear fool

Foolish cat

Flower fool

Chocolate Chip Cookies

You will need:

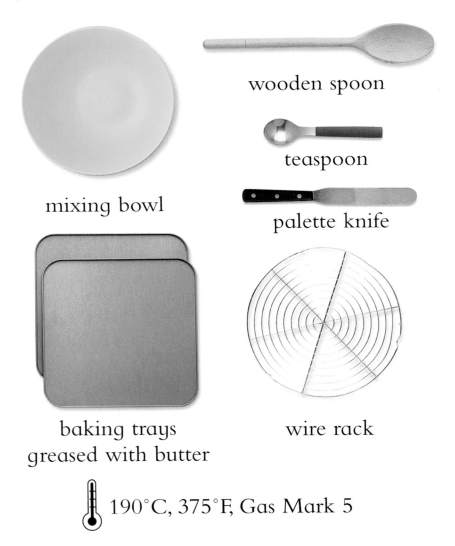

wooden spoon

teaspoon

palette knife

mixing bowl

baking trays
greased with butter

wire rack

190°C, 375°F, Gas Mark 5

To make 18 cookies, you will need:

100g (4oz)
soft butter

65g (2½oz) soft
brown sugar

65g (2½oz)
caster sugar

1 egg

125g (5oz)
plain flour

½ teaspoon of
vanilla essence

½ teaspoon of
bicarbonate of soda

150g (6oz)
chocolate chips

¼ teaspoon of salt

① Put the butter and both sugars in the mixing bowl. Use the wooden spoon to beat until soft and creamy.

② Break the egg into the bowl. Beat the mixture until it is smooth.

③ Stir in the vanilla essence. Stir in the flour, salt and bicarbonate of soda, a little at a time.

④ Add the chocolate chips and stir until they are well mixed in.

5 Use the teaspoon to put small mounds of the mixture onto the baking tray. Leave plenty of space between each cookie.

6 Bake the cookies for 10 to 12 minutes, until they are golden brown.

7 Leave the cookies on the baking tray for 1 to 2 minutes to become firm. Then use the palette knife to lift them onto the wire rack to cool.

Peppermint Creams

You will need:

whisk

2 mixing bowls

sieve

wooden spoon

baking tray lined with non-stick baking parchment

chopping board

fork

1 egg white

300g (12oz)
icing sugar

a few drops of
peppermint essence

a few drops of green
food colouring

a few drops of red
food colouring

Orange or lemon creams

Instead of using the peppermint essence and the red
and green food colouring, you can use:

a few drops of
orange juice

or a few drops of
lemon juice

a few drops of orange
food colouring

or a few drops of
yellow food colouring

1 In the large mixing bowl, whisk the egg white until it is light and frothy.

2 Sift the icing sugar into the small bowl. Then stir the sugar into the egg white, a little at a time.

3 Using your hands, roll the mixture into a ball. Make a small dip in the middle and put in the peppermint essence. Knead the essence carefully into the ball.

4 Split the mixture in three balls. Knead red food colouring evenly into one ball and gree food colouring evenly into another. Leave the last ball white.

5 For each colour, roll the mixture into small balls and put them on the baking tray. Then flatten the balls with a fork and leave them to set overnight.

Why not invite your friends to a party?

Menu

Giant Rolls

Mini Pizzas

Fruit Fools

Chocolate Chip Cookies

Peppermint Creams